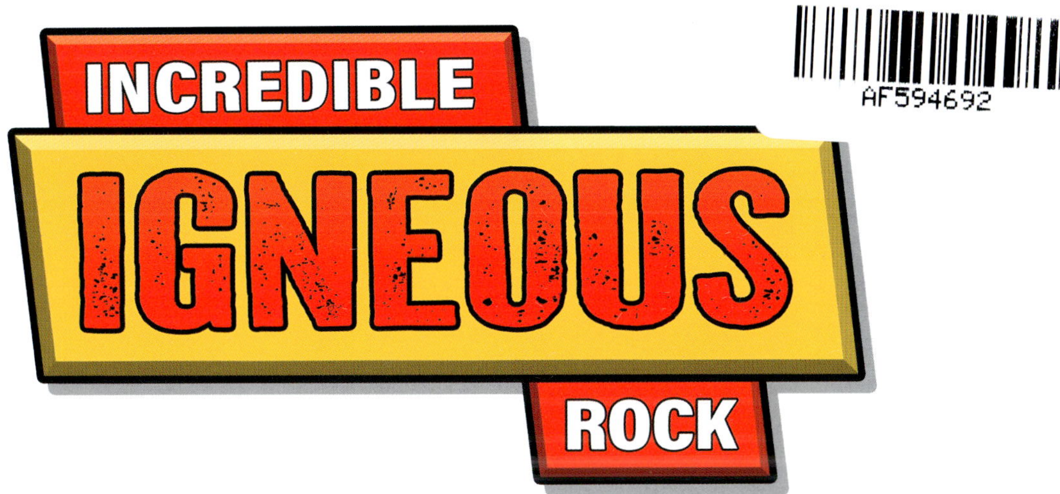

by Rex Ruby

Minneapolis, Minnesota

Credits
Cover and title page, © Probuxtor/Getty Images; 4–5, © Portra/iStock; 6–7, © Ralf Lehmann/Adobe Stock; 9, © / Shutterstock; 10, © tusharkoley/Shutterstock; 11, © /Shutterstock; 13, © /Shutterstock; 14–15, © hakanyalicn/ Shutterstock; 16–17, © jon_chica/Adobe Stock; 18T, © Bea Kiss/Shutterstock; 18B, © TR_Studio/Shutterstock; 19, © Leonid Andronov/Shutterstock; 20–21, © Wavebreakmedia/iStock; 22, © michal812/Getty Images; Used Throughout, © kyoshino/iStock.

Bearport Publishing Company Product Development Team
President: Jen Jenson; Director of Product Development: Spencer Brinker; Managing Editor: Allison Juda; Associate Editor: Naomi Reich; Associate Editor: Tiana Tran; Art Director: Colin O'Dea; Designer: Kim Jones; Designer: Kayla Eggert; Product Development Assistant: Owen Hamlin

Library of Congress Cataloging-in-Publication Data is available at www.loc.gov or upon request from the publisher.

ISBN: 979-8-89232-028-3 (hardcover)
ISBN: 979-8-89232-505-9 (paperback)
ISBN: 979-8-89232-157-0 (ebook)

For more information, write to Bearport Publishing, 5357 Penn Avenue South, Minneapolis, MN 55419.

CONTENTS

A VOLCANO ERUPTS

The ground shakes as loud booming noises fill the air. Soon, the sky is covered in smoky **ash** and the smell of **gas** is everywhere. A huge **volcano** is erupting! Superhot orange **lava** flows down the volcano's slopes and over the ground. The melted rock moves slowly, burning everything in its path.

Lava can reach a temperature of about 2,000 degrees Fahrenheit (1,200 degrees Celsius)!

Lava

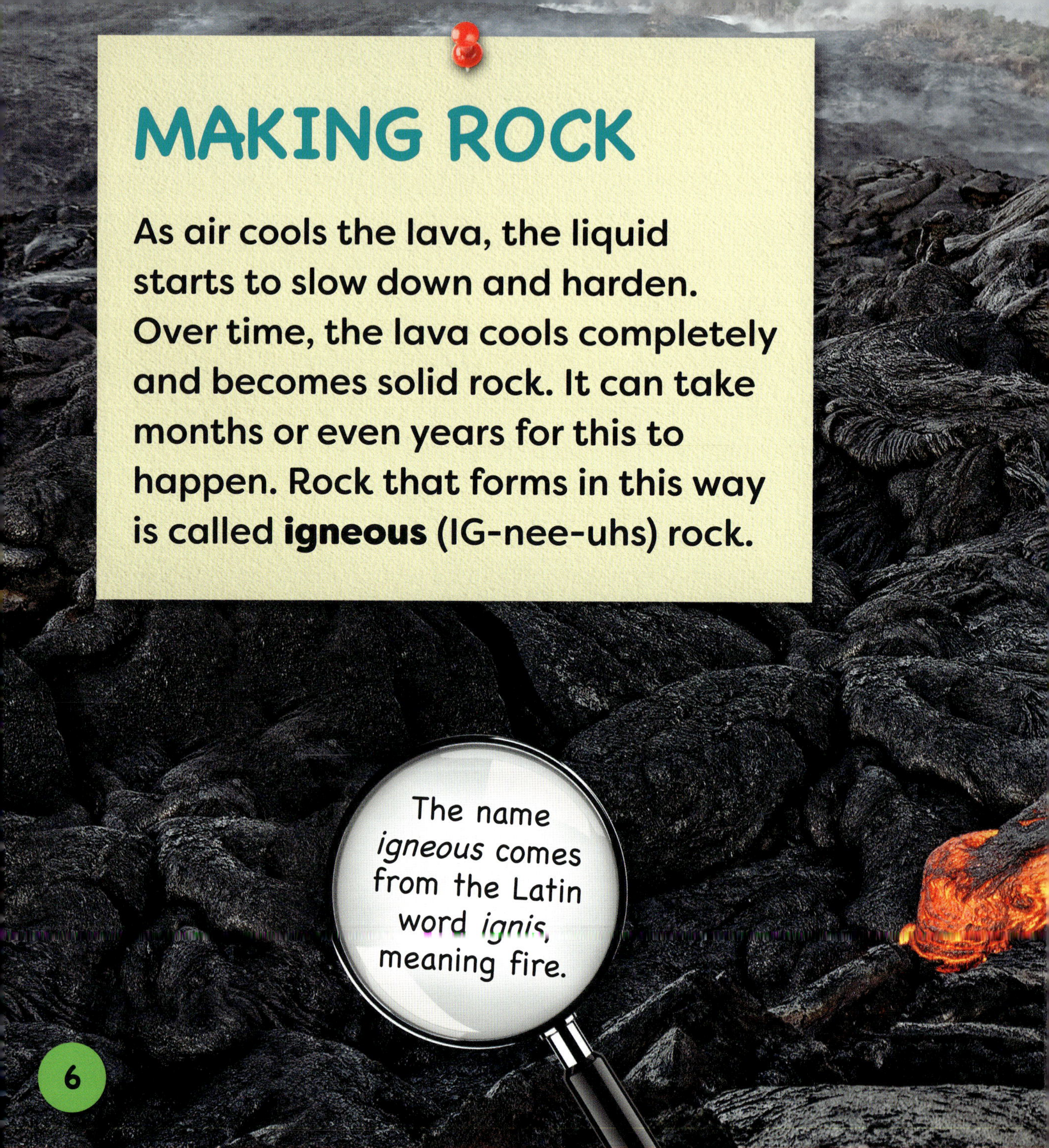

MAKING ROCK

As air cools the lava, the liquid starts to slow down and harden. Over time, the lava cools completely and becomes solid rock. It can take months or even years for this to happen. Rock that forms in this way is called **igneous** (IG-nee-uhs) rock.

The name *igneous* comes from the Latin word *ignis*, meaning fire.

After a volcanic eruption, lava slowly begins to cool down and harden.

ROCK FROM INSIDE EARTH

Where does lava come from? Beneath the planet's rocky crust, there is superhot liquid rock called **magma**. Sometimes, a crack or opening known as a volcano appears in the crust. This hole allows magma to escape onto Earth's surface. Once magma is above ground, it is known as lava.

The inside of Earth is so hot that rock deep underground actually melts into magma.

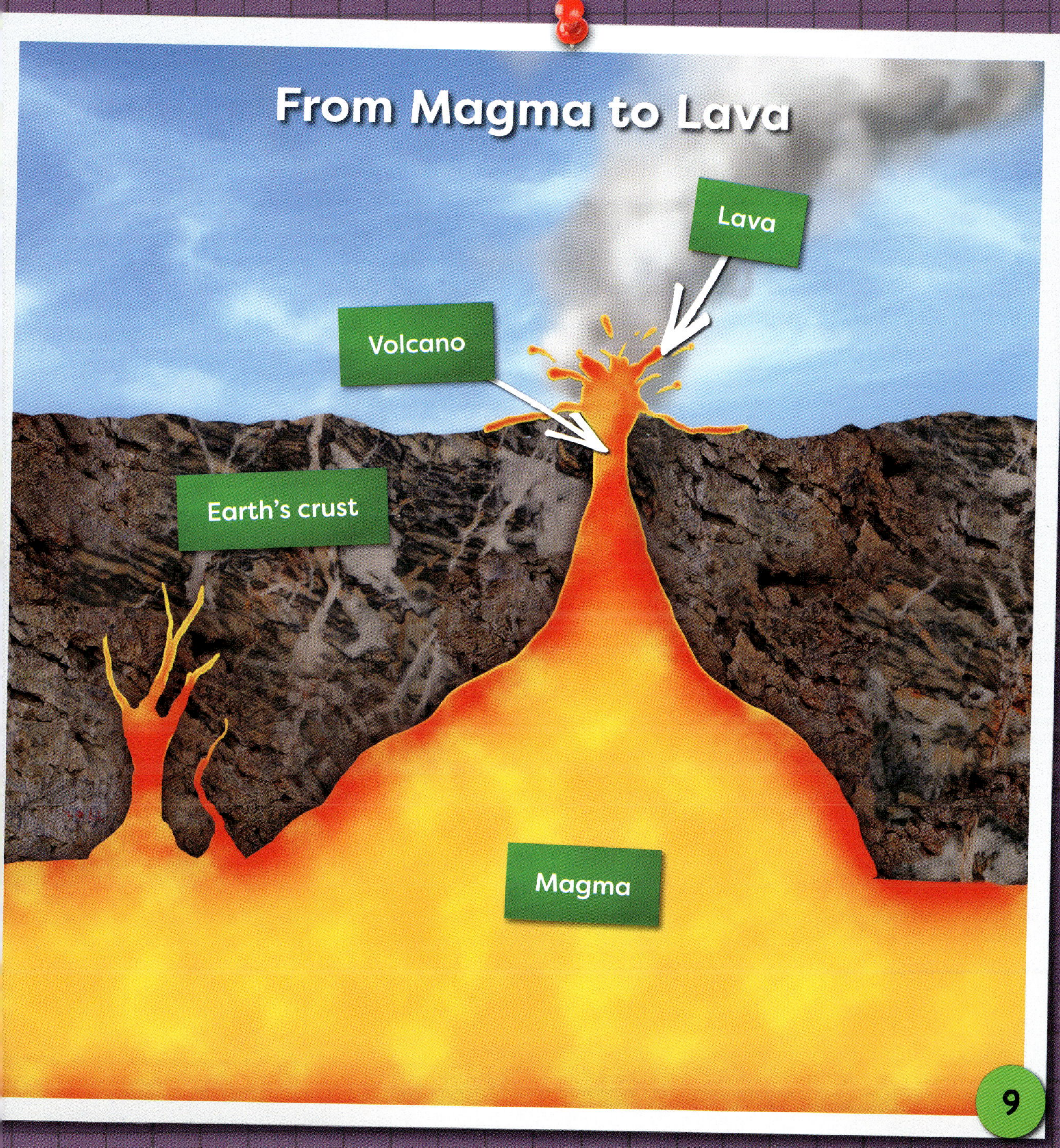
From Magma to Lava
Lava
Volcano
Earth's crust
Magma

MAKING A MOUNTAIN

When a volcano erupts, lava flows onto the ground near its opening. As the lava cools and hardens, it becomes a **mound** of igneous rock. When the volcano erupts again, more lava flows over the mound and also turns into rock. Over thousands of years, the layers of rock build up and become a mountain.

Mount Saint Helens in Washington state is a large volcano made of igneous rock.

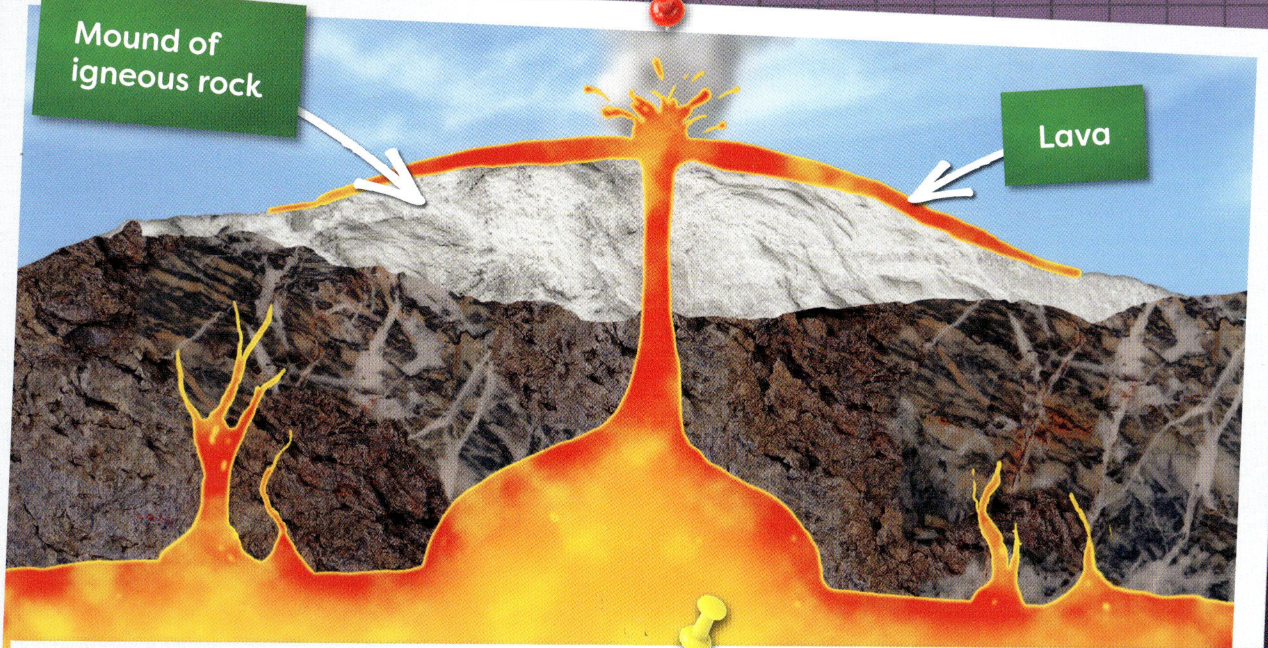

Mound of
igneous rock

Lava

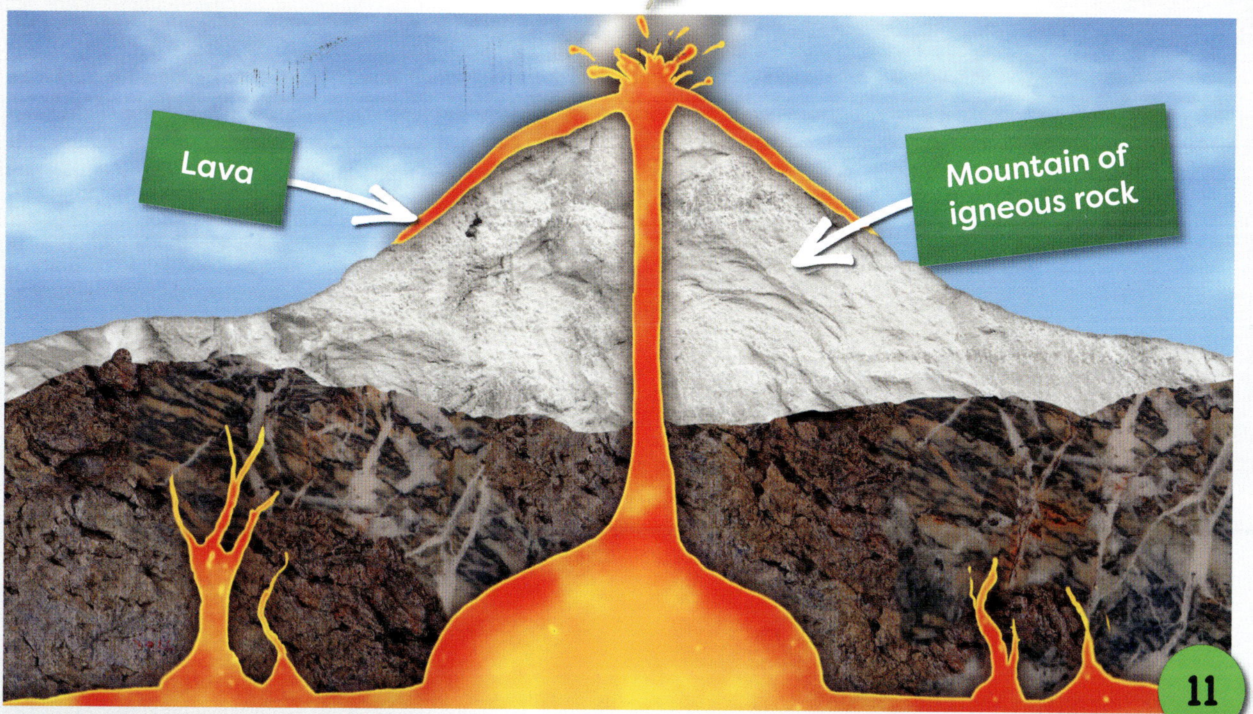

Lava

Mountain of
igneous rock

MAKING ROCK UNDERGROUND

Igneous rock isn't made only when lava makes its way to Earth's surface. It can also form inside Earth. Sometimes, cracks appear in Earth's crust deep underground. This allows magma to ooze up into the cracks. Over thousands of years, the magma cools and hardens, becoming igneous rock.

Igneous is one of the three groups of rocks. The other two are sedimentary (*sed*-uh-MEN-tur-ee), and metamorphic (*met*-uh-MOR-fik) rock.

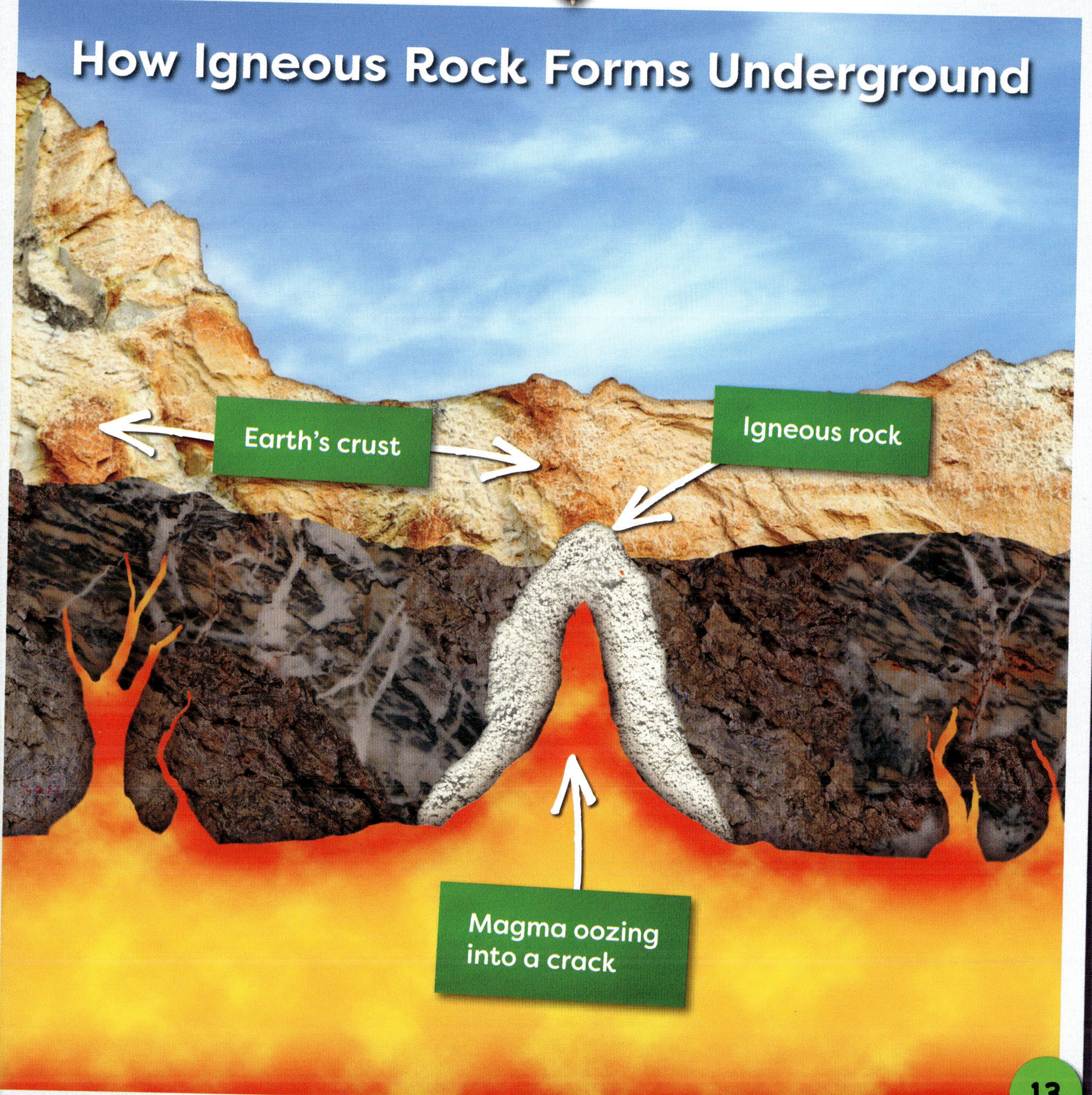
How Igneous Rock Forms Underground
Earth's crust
Igneous rock
Magma oozing into a crack

ROCKS AND MINERALS

Like all rocks, igneous rocks are made from solid substances called **minerals**. Some rocks are made from just one mineral. However, most rocks are made from a mix of different minerals. Basalt (buh-SAWLT) is an igneous rock that forms from lava on Earth's surface. The minerals inside basalt include feldspar (FELD-spaar) and olivine (AH-liv-veen).

There are more than 5,000 minerals on Earth.

A basalt cliff

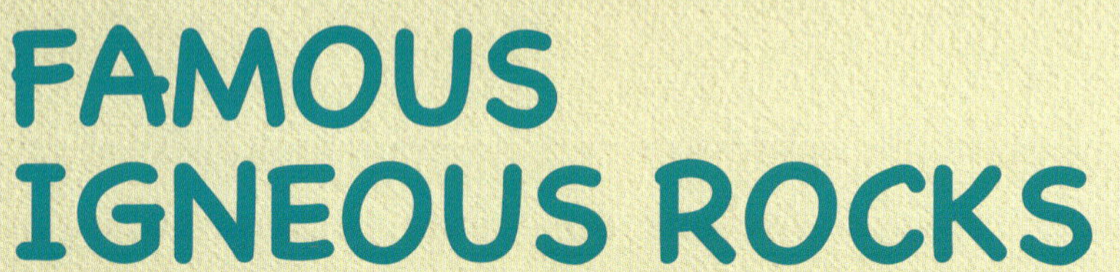

FAMOUS IGNEOUS ROCKS

There are a lot of famous rocky places made from igneous rock. One of them is the Giant's Causeway in Northern Ireland. It formed about 50 million years ago as hardening lava began to crack and break apart in strange ways. These rocks are named after an old **legend** that says they are part of a bridge built by a giant.

The Giant's Causeway is made of about 40,000 columns of basalt.

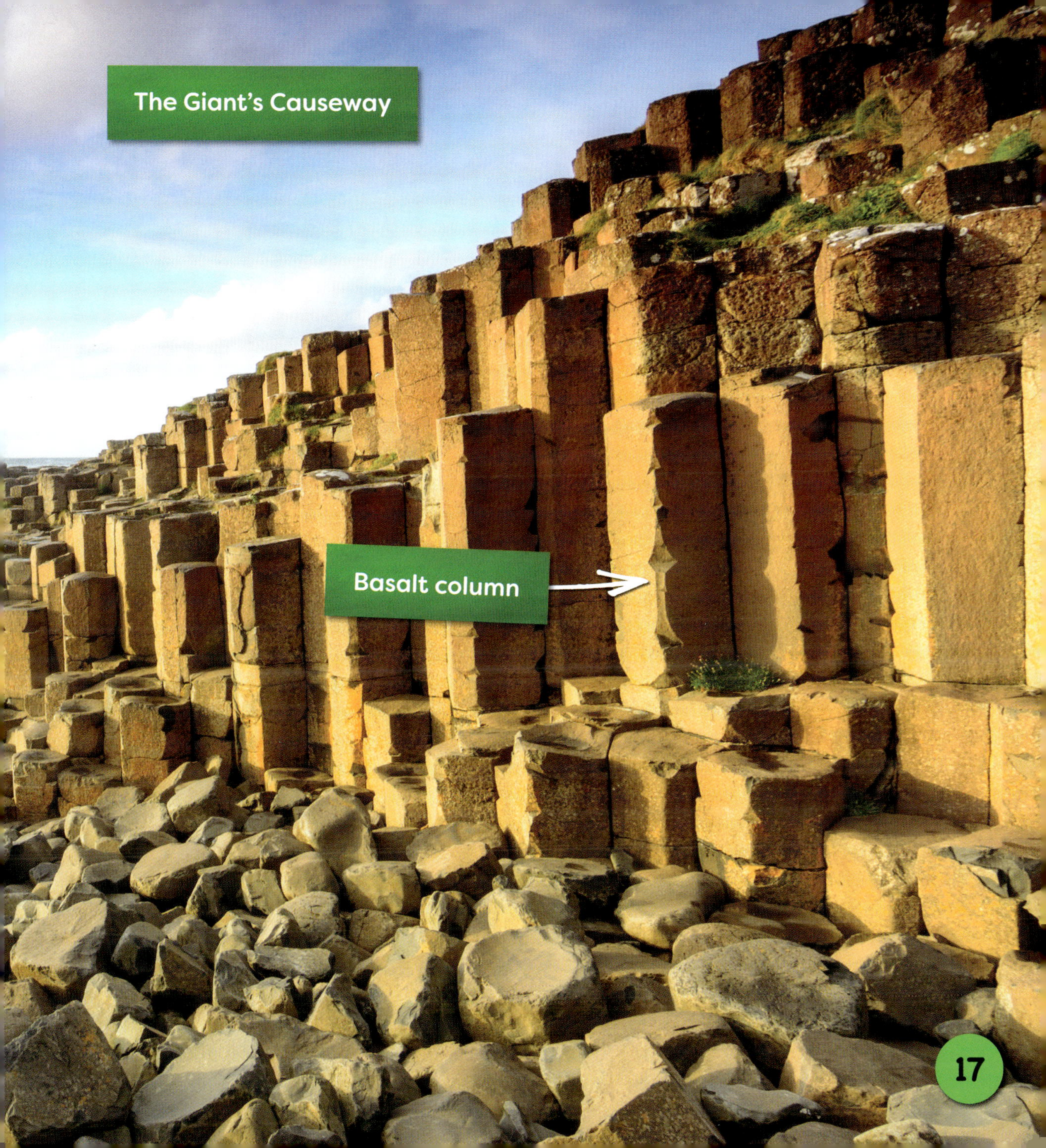
The Giant's Causeway
Basalt column

USEFUL IGNEOUS ROCKS

Igneous rocks can even be helpful to humans. Granite (GRAN-it) is an igneous rock often used in construction. People build houses, apartment buildings, and even bridges from this strong rock. Pumice (PUHM-is) is an igneous rock that is sometimes crushed and added to shower gels and soaps. The tiny grains help to scrub away dirt.

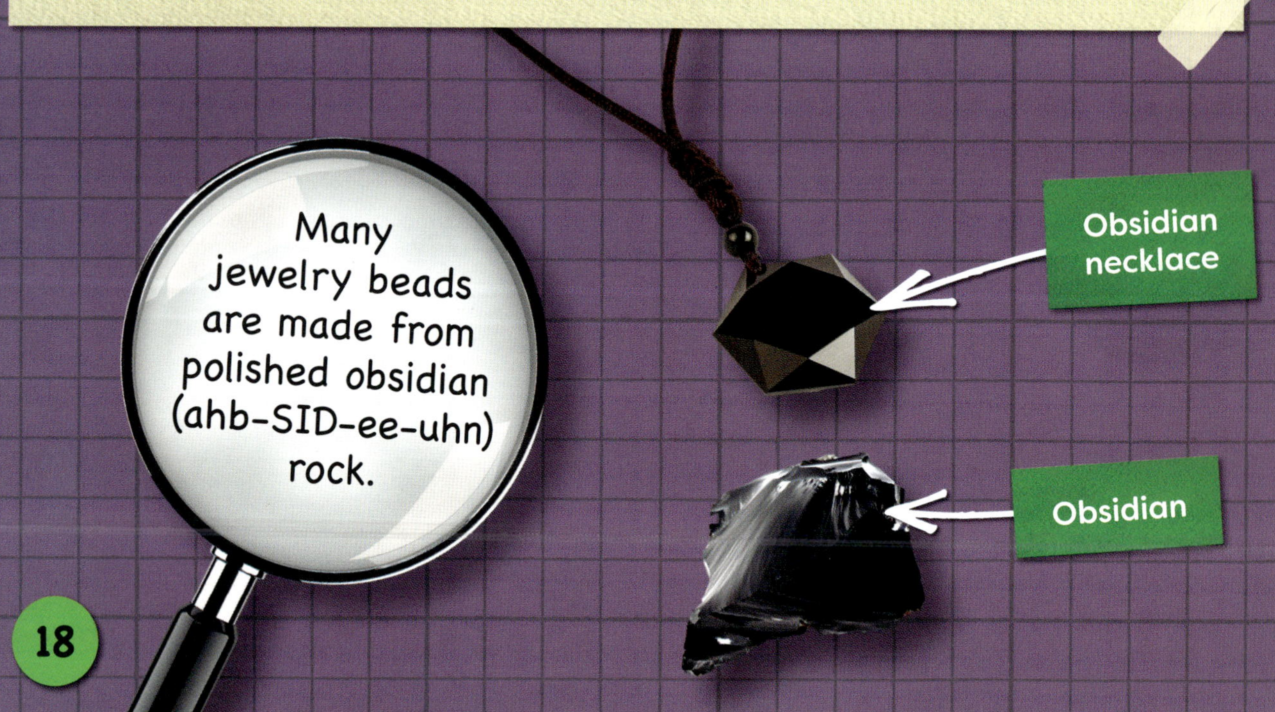

The Arlington Memorial Bridge in Washington, D.C., is made of granite.

ROCK HUNTING

For some people, finding and collecting rocks is a hobby. People who do this are called rockhounds. There are more than 700 different kinds of igneous rocks to collect. Although they formed from magma or lava, they don't all look the same. That's why rockhounds love incredible igneous rocks!

Rockhounds use books, experts, and the internet to help them **identify** the rocks they find.

SCIENCE LAB

Be a Rockhound

Become a rockhound by starting your own rock collection.

1. Look for rocks in your backyard, at the park, or at the beach. Then, sort and identify your finds!
2. Use a magnifying glass to look at your rocks more closely.
3. Identify your rocks by comparing them to pictures in books or on the internet.
4. Make labels for your rocks that include their names, where you found the rocks, and the date you found them.
5. Display your rock collection on a shelf or in a box.

GLOSSARY

ash tiny pieces of volcanic rock and minerals

gas a substance that can float in the air with no shape and that is neither liquid nor solid

identify to correctly tell what something is

igneous rock that forms from lava or magma that has cooled and become solid

lava superhot liquid rock that comes out of a volcano

legend a story handed down from long ago that may not be completely true

magma superhot liquid rock found inside Earth

minerals the solid substances found in nature that make up rocks

mound a small hill

volcano an opening in Earth's crust that allows magma from deep inside Earth to reach the surface

INDEX

READ MORE

McDougal, Anna. *Igneous Rocks (Earth's Rocks in Review)*. Buffalo, NY: Enslow Publishing, 2024.

Morlock, Rachael. *It's a Volcano Tornado! (Wildly Weird Weather)*. Buffalo, NY: Gareth Stevens Publishing, 2023.

LEARN MORE ONLINE

1. Go to **www.factsurfer.com** or scan the QR code below.
2. Enter "**Rockin Igneous**" into the search box.
3. Click on the cover of this book to see a list of websites.

ABOUT THE AUTHOR

Rex Ruby lives in Minnesota with his family. He likes going on long walks and discovering new rocks along the trail.